A Machine's View

Wimpy Kid Series

M. Max Boroumand
&
Vertias Boroumand
&
Severin Boroumand

A 2018 boroumand – A MediArt Company edition
Copyright © 2018 by M. Max Boroumand
All rights reserved.

Published in the United States by
boroumand – A MediArt Company
www.boroumand.com

Cover Design: M. Max Boroumand

Bookstore ISBN-13: 978-0-9969496-6-8
Amazon ISBN-13: 978-1-7906924-3-9

Contents

Preface

At the dinner table and frequently, my eldest would read passages of whichever of the *Diary* books he had checked out of the library. He enjoyed the books and loved making us laugh with the antics from the books. He'd read the passages as though he was a character from the book, including the voice-overs.

He got a kick out of the series, reading most of them several times each, influencing my youngest with the same passion. The two of them fought over the books, yelling, *"This is mine,"* and me reminding them both that the books belonged to the library.

I asked other parents if their children read these books with the same appetite. The answers were always, *"Yes! But I don't understand why!"* I read a few pages now and then at the same dinner table. I couldn't make time to read the books myself, too busy doing everything else!

Yet, I remained curious why my kids read them.

What is it about those books?

The question coincided with a research paper I was reading about *Artificial Intelligence (**AI**)* and *Machine Learning (**ML**).* The paper covered how, in the future, software programs would write books following the requisite machine learning process.

As an author, mathematician, and software developer I became intrigued.

Was it possible for a machine to write books?

What would it take?

How would it be done?

My plan became applying *Natural Language Processing* (**NLP**) algorithms and programs on a series of books, testing the premise.

Along the way, I would look at other aspects of the books, such as word count, N-grams, sentiment, mood, and word distribution.

A complete checkup.

The *Diary of a Wimpy Kids* collection seemed a logical series to investigate, given my children's passion. In the process of learning about them, I made this a teaching moment for my kids. The results of which follow.

Who should read this book?

I think this book would be a fun read for two groups of people. (1) Young adults who loved the series as children and those who are reading the books now. (2) Parents who then fall into two categories:

♦

Parents who want to better understand the books. These are parents who, like me, were curious about the books and why their children read them. This book will give them a little insight into the content without having to read them all.

♦

Parents who want to teach their children about the potential of Artificial Intelligence, Machine Leaning, Natural Language Processing, and Algorithms at a high level. This book would be a great tool to impart knowledge on the subject applied to something their children are enjoying - *The Diary of a Wimpy Kid books.* The process of creating this book, the journey, and the results are all worthy topics and can start conversations on these important topics.

Concepts and Definitions

Artificial Intelligence and underlying sub-topics are deep and confusing for most people. It's best if we start with a primer on some key areas from this book, offering additional reading sources and examples.

◆

Artificial Intelligence (AI)

AI, sometimes called *machine intelligence*, is intelligence showed by machines, in contrast to the *natural intelligence* displayed by humans and other animals. In 1955 John McCarthy, a young Assistant Professor of Mathematics at Dartmouth College, organized a group to clarify and develop ideas about thinking machines. He picked the name 'Artificial Intelligence' for the new field and held the first workshop on the subject at Dartmouth University in the summer of 1956. Since that day it has grown to mean many things to different people and now encompasses a broad spectrum of subfields, but its essence is still having technology doing what humans do, did, will do.

Additional Reading:

Timeline of Artificial Intelligence
(https://en.wikipedia.org/wiki/Timeline_of_artificial_intelligence)

History of Artificial Intelligence

(https://en.wikipedia.org/wiki/History_of_artificial_intelligence)

Machine Learning (ML)

ML, is a subfield of *artificial intelligence* and an interdisciplinary field that uses statistical techniques to give computer systems or software the ability to "learn" and to "improve" performance on a specific task learned from data, without it being specifically programmed into them.

Usages: Facial and Image Recognition; Smart Cars and Drones; Google Translate; Streaming Services (Netflix, Spotify, YouTube); Video Games; Online Ads; Navigation (Google Maps.)

Additional Reading:

Timeline of Machine Learning

(https://en.wikipedia.org/wiki/Timeline_of_machine_learning)

Machine Learning

(https://en.wikipedia.org/wiki/Machine_learning)

Natural language Processing (NLP)

NLP, is a subfield of computer science, information engineering, and *artificial intelligence* concerned with the interactions between computers and human (natural) languages, in particular how to program computers to process and analyze large amounts of natural language data.

Usages: Autocomplete; Predictive-Typing; Spell Checkers; Grammar Checkers; Spam Detection; Plagiarism Detection; Mood Analysis; Sentiment Analysis; Siri and OK Google; and Chatbots.

Additional Reading:

Natural Language Processing
(https://en.wikipedia.org/wiki/Natural_language_processing)

Algorithms

In mathematics and computer science, an algorithm is an explicit specification of how to solve a class of problems, and perform calculations, data processing, and automated reasoning tasks.

Usages: Encryption; Cryptography; Sorting, Ordering, and Grouping; Graph Searching and Routing (FedEX, UPS, USPS); Link Analysis and Ranking (Google Search); Data Compression (Netflix, Spotify); Facial Recognition and Image Recognition; ... Thousands more, everywhere.

Additional Reading:

Algorithms
(https://en.wikipedia.org/wiki/Algorithm)

List of Algorithms

(https://en.wikipedia.org/wiki/List_of_algorithms)

Optical Character Recognition (OCR)

OCR, Is the mechanical or electronic conversion of images of typed, handwritten or printed text into machine-encoded text, whether from a scanned document, a photo of a document, a scene-photo (for example the text on signs and billboards in a landscape photo) or from subtitle text superimposed on an image (for example from a television broadcast).

Usages: Scanners; Smart Phones; License Plate Readers; Google Mapping Cars;

Parsing

The term has different meanings in different branches of linguistics and computer science. Traditional sentence parsing is often performed as a method of understanding the exact meaning of a sentence or word, sometimes with the aid of devices such as sentence diagrams. It emphasizes the importance of grammatical divisions such as subject and predicate. Within *computational linguistics*, they use the term to refer to the formal analysis by a computer of a sentence or other string of words into its constituents, resulting in a parse tree showing their syntactic relation to each other, which may also contain semantic and other information. They also use the term in *psycholinguistics* when describing language comprehension. In this book, parsing refers to how human beings analyze a sentence or phrase, in spoken language or text.

Usages: Breaking a sentence down to a collection of words; extracting an area code from a phone number sequence; Code Analysis; Language Analysis and Translation;

Additional Reading:

Parsing (https://en.wikipedia.org/wiki/Parsing)

Vectorization

In **ML** and **AI**, vectorization is the term for converting a *scalar* program to a *vector* program so that programs can run multiple operations from a single instruction, while scalar programs can only operate on pairs of operands at once. This is important in **ML** and **AI** because it allows for computers that have **GPUs** to outperform **CPUs**. In simple terms, it allows you to replace a set of many iterative looped calculations, with a single calculation; or, the process of converting an algorithm from operating on a single value at a time to operating on a set of values (vector) at one time.

Usages: Machine Learning Neural Networks; Linear Algebra;

Additional Reading:

Vectorization in Mathematics
(https://en.wikipedia.org/wiki/Vectorization_(mathematics))

Array Programming
(https://en.wikipedia.org/wiki/Array_programming)

CPU versus GPU

The *Central Processing Unit* (**CPU**) is the brains of the PC. The *Graphics Processing Unit* (**GPU**) supports 3D game and image rendering. These days, GPUs are broadly used to speed up computational workloads in areas such as **AI** and **ML**. Where a **CPU** may have dual-cores or quad-cores, a **GPU** may have thousands of cores, allowing for massive parallel processing.

Word Cloud

A World Cloud is a visual representation of text, typically used to depict keyword metadata (tags) in documents or websites, or to visualize free form text. Tags are usually single words, and the importance of each tag is shown with font size or color.

n-Grams

In the fields of *computational linguistics* and **NLP**, an n-gram is a contiguous sequence of n items from a sample of text or speech. The items can be phonemes, syllables, letters, words, or base pairs according to the application (e.g., 'I Love you.' (3-gram), 'To be or not to be' (6-gram.)

Usages: Language and Style modelling; Predicative Typing; Mood and Sentiment Analysis; and Grade Level Analysis.

Additional Reading:

n-grams (https://en.wikipedia.org/wiki/N-gram)

Lexical Diversity

Lexical Diversity is the ratio of different unique word stems (types) to the total number of words (tokens). The term is used in *Applied Linguistics* and *NLP* fields as an equivalent to *lexical richness*, and should include a blend of Variability, Volume, Evenness, Rarity, Dispersion, and Disparity. The better the blend, for each specific age group and genre, the better the writing.

Usages: Grade Level Analysis; Writing Comparative Analysis;

Epoch

An epoch is one complete presentation of the data set to be learned to a learning machine. Learning machines, like feed-forward neural nets that use iterative algorithms, often need many epochs during their learning phase.

Neural Networks

This topic requires a much deeper look beyond the simple primer in the previous chapter. *Neural Networks* (***NN***) are the foundation for many of the **ML** and **AI** efforts out there.

So what exactly are they?

neu.ral net.work (*noun*)
A computer system modeled on the human brain and nervous system.

NN are inspired by the biological neural networks that make up the brain. They are not algorithms, but rather a framework for different learning algorithms to work together processing complex data inputs. Such systems learn by considering and studying examples, without being programmed to follow any prescribed process or steps. A popular example of its usage is image recognition. The ability to learn from examples, just as we humans do, to identify, and differentiate between objects, people, or animals (e.g., cats v. dogs, circles v. squares, Uncle Bob v. Aunt Sally.)

An **NN** is based on a collection of connected ***nodes*** called artificial neurons, which loosely model the neurons in a biological brain. Each connection, like the synapses in a biological brain, can transmit a signal from one artificial neuron to another. An artificial neuron that receives a signal can process it and then signal additional artificial neurons connected to it.

The best way to explain this is to build a simple image recognition **NN** that distinguishes between images of Zeros (0) and Ones (1), skipping the complex math mind you.

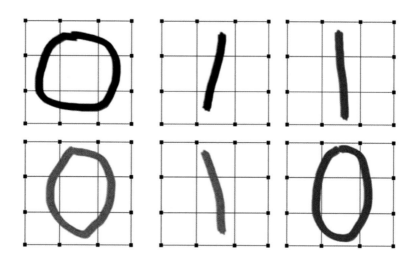

Let's train our machine to distinguish between 0 and 1 given a 3x3 pixel training set, by first breaking the pictures down to their 9 unique parts (a 3 by 3 matrix) where each pixel will be an input into the learning system.

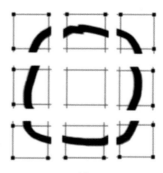

With each picture properly labeled as either a "one" or a "zero," and offering nine unique inputs into the learning machine, we get the following **NN**.

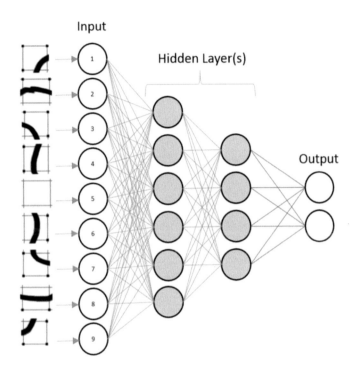

Every **NN** has:

- One Input layer of nodes,

- One or more hidden layers of nodes, and

- One Output or result layer with nodes.

The ***input layer*** has as many nodes as there are features you are to evaluate. In our example, we have nine pixels each with information, or a feature of the number's shape.

Fun Fact

In facial recognition, there are 128 features extracted from an image called an **embedding**. To build an NN classifier will require 128 input 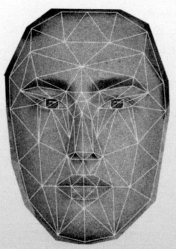 nodes that allow it to learn who's who. Once you have taught the NN to associate a name to the embedding, you can feed it any image and if you have a name in the database, it will pop out a result for you.

The **hidden layers** are where you conduct your learning. They are detectors of sorts. It is where you, at each node, assign different weights based on what you detect, and where each layer could focus on one attribute. For example, one layer could learn about numbers, another about colors, and so on. So in our **NN** diagram above we can say the first hidden layer learns about ones and zeros, and the second learns about the colors black, blue, and red. The number of hidden layers and nodes in an **NN** are a function of the learning model, trial and error, and other model based distinctions.

Finally, we have an **output layer** with two output nodes, representing a *Zero* or *One* (*or*, six output nodes, representing Black 0, Black 1, Red 0, Red 1, Blue 0, and Blue 1.)

◆

An **NN** works by taking as input many labeled data, *The Learning Set*. In our example, images of zeros and ones labeled as *Red 1*, *Blue 0*, *Black 0*, etc. After studying the learning set, the **NN** creates a matrix of weights for each hidden layer that corresponds with what it has learned, and over time, it readjusts those weights with new information as it learns further. Once we train the **NN**, it is ready to take as input the *Test Set*, which is data without the labels. We don't know what numbers or colors they are. The desired output would be the missing labels. Once tested and tuned, we can now use our **NN** to identify zeros and ones.

Fun Fact

In an NN, the hidden layers and the nodes in each layer are compared to the neurons in a brain and how they are connected to each other. An NN mimics the way a brain works, looking at parts and pieces, back and forth, forming relationships, and conclusions in order to learn.

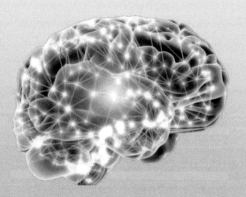

However, the similarity is a loose inspirational one only. The mammalian brain contains between 100 million and 100 billion neurons, depending on the species.

Neural Networks use a variety of models (e.g., Convolutional, Feed Forward, Recurrent, Modular, Radial Basis Function, Kohonen Self Organizing, etc.) used in **ML** to do:

- Speech Recognition

- Computer Vision (e.g., radiology)

- Electric and Power Grid Restoration

- Pattern Recognition (e.g., Disease Identification.)

- Text to Speech

- Text Generation

- Image Classification

We will use a Neural Network to generate our text at the end of the book. But before we do that, let's look at the process and some of our findings along the way.

The Process

I chose the first ten diaries as a sample set and a good starting point for my project. Each book had around 210± pages with each page being a combination of words and sketches.

The books I used were the following ten:

#	Book	Year
1	Diary of a Wimpy Kid	2007
2	Rodrick Rules	2008
3	The Last Straw	2009
4	Dog Days	2009
5	The Ugly Truth	2010
6	Cabin Fever	2011
7	The Third Wheel	2012
8	Hard Luck	2013
9	The Long Haul	2014
10	Old School	2015

Step One – Convert Images to Text

With the digital versions in hand, the process of sentence and word extraction began. The books were *not* in text format. Each page was an image that made Optical Character Recognition (**OCR**) more difficult and messy. **OCR** works great if the input is clean and geometrically precise. However, in this case the text was more akin to handwriting. Then there were sketches with speech bubbles and randomly drawn words.

Most **OCRs** I tested netted a collection of garbage. Google's natural language processes had the best algorithms resulting in excellent outputs with errors in the low single digits.

Most errors occurred when the algorithms deciphered the sketches. Errors fell into two categories, which I'll call *Crumbs* and *Trains*. We manually parsed both error groups to be sure we collected all the words.

- **Crumbs** (e.g., *a, oa, at, now*, etc.) are single, two, or three character words that could either be a word or not. And even if it was a word, it may not have been one from the book, but a word converted.

- **Trains** are those where the **OCR** couldn't split the word (e.g., *MomandDadwerevery.*)

With the words and sentences extracted. The real work began.

Step Two – *Strip Away Non-Essentials*

The stripping process entailed removal of all numbers, punctuations, and non-ASCII characters. And included the conversion of all words to lower-case so that words such as "dad" and "Dad" fell within the same equal set.

Stripping netted flaws. For example, the removal of the apostrophe changing words like "can't" to "can" and "t" which effected the word count and the sentiment analysis. I corrected those words and regrouped them.

Step Three – *Parsing and Vectorization*

With the data in raw format, we parsed further, putting the words in tables, including the corrected trains and crumbs. The trains had to be broken up into separate words. Once in the tables, I had a script run the words against a dictionary to remove all non-words.

Parsing and cleanup netted more flaws. Not all crumbs were removed, and the process removed certain good words. I rectified these flaws and reinserted those words back into the tables. The process was not perfect and I am sure I missed words here and there.

Step Four – *Begin Analysis*

With all the words sorted and organized, the analysis began.

I began by creating and examining word clouds for each book. Followed by looking at word size frequency and at the largest words in each book.

I continued the process by examining n-grams, conducting high-level sentiment analysis, and then finishing with some keyword distributions and density across the ten books.

I finished by building a neural network and having a machine write the new text based on the 10 books as the learning set. *My original goal!*

◆

Here are the results...

Words

Clouds

My first pass at the collection of words was to study them as *Word Clouds*.

However, in order to get an informative cloud, I removed common words, (e.g., 'to' at 6504± and 'of' at 3295± occurrences.)

The first cloud we created, without the common words, had the word 'out' as the largest word at 1422± surpassing 'mom' at 1329±. We removed that but kept the word 'just' as I believed it meaningful in a child's usage of the word.

Most Word Cloud algorithms have their own word parsing and grouping approaches resulting in clouds that were not under

our direct control. So for each we bypassed their algorithms and provided our own lists. We merely used them to draw the images.

Word Size Frequency

The next view of words was one of size. A view of the number of characters in the words, (e.g., go (2), mom (3), gone (4), etc.) I removed the two character words, as they were too numerous and included some crumbs, throwing off the chart.

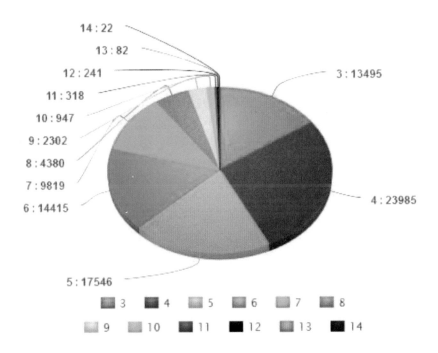

The largest words had fourteen characters (e.g. *kindergartners, responsibility*.) Although there were a few larger hyphenated words, those were broken into their parts and counted separately.

Words with four characters topped the chart at 23,985± occurrences.

Here are the top twenty words from the cloud. Mom showed up 342± times more often than dad, or 25% more. The contraction didn't occurred 525± times and the adverb just 525± times. I see both in defensive or contractual arguments: *I didn't do that*; *I didn't think of that*; *Just a little more time*; or, *I just want to play.*

Word	Count	Word	Count
Mom	1317±	Really	654±
Dad	975±	Time	622±
Got	954±	School	558±
Get	906±	Back	553±
Rowley	812±	Didn't	525±
Just	798±	Told	496±
Said	764±	Thing	446±
One	757±	Even	406±
Rodrick	705±	Gonna	403±
Like	704±	Think	403±

Most popular words…

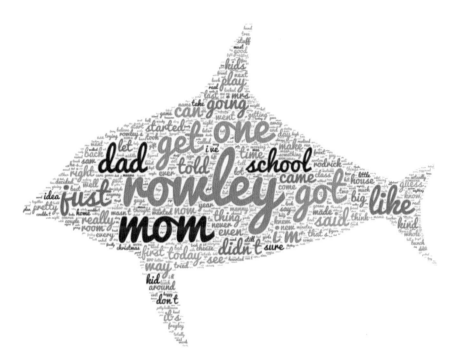

Biggest words…

Word	Count	Word	Count
Kindergarteners	5±	Enthusiastic	3±
Disappointment	1±	Refrigerator	3±
Unfortunately	7±	Encyclopedia	2±
Embarrassment	2±	Kindergarten	1±
Brainstorming	1±	Specifically	1±
Announcement(s)	5±	Expectations	1±
Concentration	1±	Disappointment	1±
Advertisement	1±	Contributors	1±
Butterfingers	1±	Disrespected	1±
Neighborhood	7±	Accidentally	1±

Most popular words…

Biggest words …

Word	Count	Word	Count
Responsibility	1±	Presentations	1±
Questionnaires	1±	Accidentally	7±
Accomplishment	1±	Thanksgiving	6±
Kindergartners	1±	Embarrassing	5±
Congratulating	1±	Professional	4±
Unfortunately	1±	Neighborhood	3±
Stealthinator	1±	Refrigerator	2±
Ventriloquist	1±	Infiltrating	1±
Kindergartner	1±	Relationship	1±
Grandchildren	1±	Accomplished	1±

Most popular words …

Biggest words …

Word	Count	Word	Count
Congratulations	1±	Enthusiastic	4±
Unfortunately	3±	Instructions	2±
Concentrating	1±	Accidentally	2±
Embarrassment	1±	Concentrated	2±
TenderCuddles	1±	Disappointed	2±
Ventriloquism	1±	Consequences	2±
Professionals	1±	Intelligence	1±
Circumstances	1±	Professional	1±
Conversation	7±	Benchwarmers	1±
Neighborhood	1±	Speakerphone	1±

Most popular words …

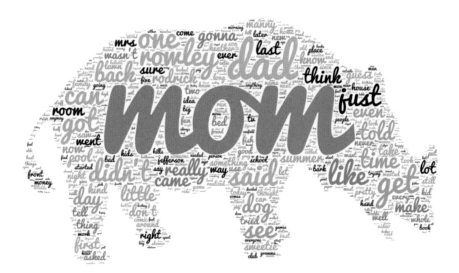

Biggest words …

Word	Count	Word	Count
Transportation	4±	Specifically	2±
Unfortunately	9±	Conversation	2±
Entertainment	4±	Announcement	2±
Relationships	2±	Refrigerator	2±
Unpredictable	1±	Accidentally	2±
Uncomfortable	1±	Togetherness	2±
Concentrating	1±	Instructions	1±
Neighborhood	4±	Illustration	1±
Embarrassing	2±	Constipation	1±
Relationship	2±	Competition	6±

Most popular words …

Biggest words …

Word	Count	Word	Count
Misunderstanding	1±	Antibacterial	1±
Responsibility	5±	Autobiography	1±
Transformation	2±	Congratulated	1±
Unfortunately	11±	Opportunities	1±
Uncomfortable	4±	Kindergarten	3±
Clarification	4±	Disappointed	3±
Parallelogram	3±	Refrigerator	3±
Troublemakers	2±	Neighborhood	2±
Inappropriate	2±	Embarrassing	2±
Disrespectful	1±	Disqualified	2±

Book #6 | Cabin Fever

Most popular words …

Biggest words …

Word	Count	Word	Count
Responsibility	1±	Thanksgiving	5±
Multiplication	1±	Embarrassing	3±
Unfortunately	5±	Disappointed	3±
Uncomfortable	1±	Kindergarten	2±
Announcements	1±	Presidential	2±
Troublemakers	1±	Schneiderman	2±
Circumstances	1±	Unidentified	2±
Entertainment	1±	Perpetrators	1±
Inappropriate	1±	Unauthorized	1±
Neighborhood	13±	Refrigerator	1±

Most popular words …

Biggest words …

Word	Count	Word	Count
Kindergartners	5±	Announcement	4±
Disappointment	1±	Enthusiastic	3±
Unfortunately	7±	Refrigerator	3±
Embarrassment	2±	Encyclopedia	3±
Brainstorming	1±	Intelligence	2±
Announcements	1±	Accidentally	1±
Advertisement	1±	Kindergarten	1±
Butterfingers	1±	Contributors	1±
Concentration	1±	Disrespected	1±
Neighborhood	7±	Cheerleaders	1±

Most popular words …

Biggest words …

Word	Count	Word	Count
Congratulations	1±	Neighborhood	4±
Responsibility	2±	Photographer	4±
Accomplishment	1±	Caterpillars	2±
Unfortunately	8±	Accidentally	2±
International	1±	Relationship	2±
Personalizing	1±	Kindergarten	2±
Automatically	1±	Disqualified	1±
Metamorphosis	1±	Conversation	1±
Skateboarding	1±	Construction	1±
Sophisticated	1±	Concentrated	1±

Most popular words …

Biggest words …

Word	Count	Word	Count
Disappointment	1±	Concentrating	4±
Unfortunately	5±	Conditioning	4±
Uncomfortable	2±	Conversation	4±
Antibacterial	1±	Accidentally	3±
Veterinarian(s)	7±	Embarrassing	3±
Investigation	1±	Intersection	2±
Immunizations	1±	Receptionist	2±
Communicating	1±	Consequences	1±
Undergarments	1±	Registration	1±
International	1±	Civilization	1±

Most popular words ...

Biggest words ...

Word	Count	Word	Count
Overprotective	2±	Imaginations	2±
Simultaneously	1±	Accidentally	2±
Establishments	1±	Embarrassing	2±
Unfortunately	6±	Overpowering	1±
Uncomfortable	3±	Disappointed	1±
Experimenting	1±	Conditioning	1±
Relationships	1±	Toothbrushes	1±
Troublemakers	1±	Instructions	1±
Hardscrabble	17±	Professional	1±
Neighborhood	3±	Consequences	1±

Natural Language Processing

Having looked at the words by themselves, their count and size, next we looked at the natural language, words in collections, and sentiments. We used Stanford's Natural Language Processing tools and software to organize and categorize the words in their native and original form.

You may interpret as you see fit.

Sentiment Analysis | N-grams

In the field of natural language analysis, sequences are given a positive, negative, or neutral score that in summation may reflect sentiment.

For example, in evaluating reviews for a book you may use the following small subset:

n-gram	score	n-gram	score
I Hate	-2	I Love	+2
I Dislike	-1	I Like	+1
It's alright	0	It's Fine	0

Processing thousands of reviews using n-grams can quickly give you a good understanding of where things stand. The scoring models can be as complex as you wish and can entail dimensions beyond mere good or bad.

N-grams are also used to study writing styles, educational level, country of origin, inclinations, readability, and much more.

In the ten books analyzed, these are the most popular two word n-grams, 2-grams:

2-grams	Count
I don't	175±
I didn't	173±
I couldn't	91±
I wasn't	71±
I'm not	65±
Didn't have	65±

And, the most popular 3-grams:

3-grams	Count
A bunch of	136±
Me and Rowley	134±
I had to	125±
Out of the	124±
Mom and dad	123±
The rest of	120±

And, the most popular 4-grams.

4-grams	Count
The rest of the	69±
In the middle of	42±
To be honest with	41±
For the rest of	39±
To go to the	34±
And stuff like that	30±

Finally, the most popular 5-grams.

5-grams	Count
To be honest with you	41±
Be honest with you I	36±
All I can say is	19±
In the back of the	17±
But I don't think I	16±

I looked at each of the n-grams within the context of conversations I've had with my boys or one's I've heard other parents have with their children. There is a lot to derive in the way kids speak and craft sentences.

What do you think when you hear a sentence start with *"To be honest with you?"* The book's sentiments were generally positive and where negative it was in light of what kids might say or do.

Keep in mind …

Context is everything.

Word Distribution and Lexical Diversity

I like looking at certain n-grams, their usage, and frequency across all the books: *How often they are used? What are their distribution across a series? Are they used more in the first book versus the middle versus the last? Or, are they infrequent? And, in what context are they used?*

For this, we looked at the lexical diversity dispersion plot for a series of words, across all 214,433± words in ten books.

The motivation behind using the dispersion plots was to give us an alternative means of visualizing how prevalent certain words are, how they are clustered, and whether they show any theme.

Kill shows up 7± times. But, should we worry about the context? Sad shows up 13± times. Should we worry about that? Or, is it normal?

Hate shows up 14± times, all in a reasonable context.

'Hate' in Context
"Rodrick knows how much I *hate* it"
"I *hate* to say it but mom's prediction about"
"Me and dad *hate* lots of the same things "
"Rodrick knows I *hate* watercress salad"

Let's look at Kill in context.

A negatively connoted word is not what it seems, and must be looked at and scored given perspective.

Let's look at the word Sad (13±).

'Sad' in Context
"One of the things mom was really sad about ...." "Mom seemed pretty sad the trip was getting ..." "I didn't even have time to feel sad about it "I tried to think of something really sad but ..."

What about the word Happy (125±)?

'Happy' in Context
" ... dad must have been pretty happy with himself " ... was probably really happy he got such a great " ... Mom didn't seem too happy with what I said " ... we made dad pretty happy but I ..."

The negative words were normal in context.
It's all good.

We conducted word frequency and distribution, across all the books. Here is the distribution of some words across the ten books.

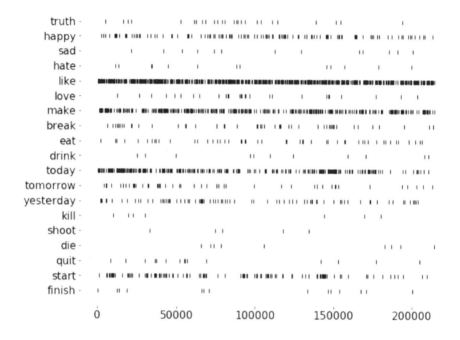

Happy is used more often than Sad and is evenly distributed.

Like is heavily used across all books, whereas Hate is rarely used as is the word Love.

Similarly, Make is used heavily and uniformly across all books, but Break is rarely used.

♦

You could spend days analyzing all the n-grams, measuring textual diversity, standard deviations of words per type, their dispersion, and disparity. But all of that is part and parcel of a more sophisticated analysis and not for this book.

The stories have a positive tone across all books. The books are a fun read, with the story sequences a normal part of the lives of many kids.

They are good books

What My Kids Say

I was curious what my boys thought of the books and if they had any advice for me on lessons learned, and whatever else I could extract from them through a Q&A session.

Me – *How many of the books have you read?*

Veritas (11) – *All of them. All ten.*
Severin (9) – *Me too. All of them.*

♦

Me – *How many have you read more than once?*

V – *All of them.*
S – *All of them.*

♦

Me – *Why read them multiple times?*

V – *I enjoyed the humor and got trapped in the book.*
S – *I enjoy how he's funny and messes up at times and is a failure sometimes. It was good to see what life could be like for others.*

Me – *Do you have a favorite book? Why?*

V – "Rodrick Rules". Because it's about an older brother and a little brother. This book focused on the brothers.

S – "Cabin Fever". It's a fun and exciting book because they are stuck in a cabin and it seems more like a little prison of adventure. A survival book.

V – Come to think of it. That too is one of my favorites. It's a more dramatic story with survival scenes. It's a lot more adventurous.

♦

Me – *Who is your favorite character and why?*

V – "Greg". He is the main character and who is telling the story. I like his voice.

S – "Greg." Same reason.

♦

Me – Who's your least favorite and why?

V – "Rodrick". He is a jerk.
S – The "Dad". He is lazy, lies often, and is not the kind of dad I would want.

♦

Me – Have you learned anything from these books?

V – No. Nothing.
S – Nothing.
Me – Nothing at all?
V – Yes, nothing. The books has no teaching value at all.
Me – Really?
S – Yes.
V – Yes.

♦

Me – Did you learn any fun pranks or tricks?

V – Probably. And I might pull some on friends.
S – Some. Not pranks, but tricks for costumes and such.

Me – Would girls enjoy these books?

V – Probably not. There is a series called "Dork Diaries" they would enjoy more.

S – Yes, because the humor gives the girls something to laugh at and is about a kid that is sort of a failure, and they may get a kick out of that.

Me – Should parents read these books?

V – If they want.

S – Probably not. Because parents should teach their kids better things than these books offer.

Me – Would you recommend them to your cousins and close friends?

V – Yes. Because the books are funny and you will get hooked very quickly.

S – Yah, because they might like the books and you can laugh about the stories together.

♦

Me – Did the books impact you? How?

V – Yes. They taught me not to be like Greg.

S – Yes. They taught me not to be like Rodrick. He is a bully and not liked.

Me – Why not like Greg?

V – He is a failure. He's not smart, makes bad mistakes and decisions. And, when he tries to fix things, he makes them worse every time.

Me - Anything good about Greg?

V – Not that I could think of but he has one friend that may find something good about him.

♦

Me – Any other questions you think parents should ask?

V – No.

S – No.

In listening to my kids, I realized one thing. Both understood the books for what they were – *Entertainment*. They didn't search for lessons, advice, guidance, or anything of the kind. That made me happy.

I spent a lot of time listening to my kids read passages, laughing the whole time. They read and re-read the books and enjoyed them. As siblings, they would often chat about parts and pieces, story lines, and whole books, again laughing and enjoying their time together.

I find the books, and the way it makes the kids want to read and read again, a positive aspect of the series. And best of all, it gives the readers a common set of events about which they can chat, laugh, and communicate.

The Machine Writes

Finally, I set upon trying to teach the machine how to write similar passages and sentences to those found within the ten books.

I put together all the programs and scripts (i.e., Keras high-level neural network APIs on top of Tensorflow libraries), and decided on 60 epochs, a small number, but a good start. I ran the program on my computer and left to get a fresh cup of coffee. Back at my desk a little later, I saw the estimated completion time calculated at six weeks.

Six weeks? That's crazy.

I didn't have time nor could I leave my computer alone for that long. That was a setback and the first major lesson in **ML** and **AI**. To do the job right, one needs massive computing power. My desktop was not the machine to use. I couldn't even run one epoch efficiently.

What to do?

I would not be dissuaded from having a machine write something for me. I looked into buying a machine for that purpose, and in doing the research I decided on building my own from parts lying around the house. What I needed was a PC case, a strong power supply, a motherboard and CPU chip (less than five years old), all of which I had. The only missing item was a new GPU, which I bought. So for the cost of less than $300 dollars and parts around the house, a week later I had my little AI machine.

I installed the Ubuntu operating system on it, added the requisite **ML** and **AI** programs, libraries, and APIs, and within hours after assembly, it was working. I transferred the data and my scripts, and re-ran my original epochs. This time around, the estimated time was six hours.

Yay!

I was not extremely happy with my first educational endeavor teaching the machine by way of 60 epochs. My machine did not learn anything. Here is what my machine wrote. After epoch 1, with seed = "end up with a couple of things he", my machine wrote:

*"actugrv cirelnnfl r wh t e euut d ntm o rtte htidrg t eni r e o e s t i acg tagnennnar e trgunw oemr eo h oerrn o el e on t u e lary e i torney htweynna hon a k h e tew e oen enon **that** hwu eti onee e ee tee ek fpstn hwur f e eutrnl r u vu un **in** w eu hmee ot oc we st inrn te re nnu e eun u wenvusu e vo thlvit enu e edsurr ttr ee u tf oer uurn t hho o sur ttu trerwvtuyrtnn mhontu"*

After epoch 60, with seed = "time and at the wrong field", my machine wrote:

"I asr i i geavvd ydaio shor rs kon ens siurtordtttloaecgwvutsdr i uy tanotu es vrrad daasrytdtnnaxvh a iittoioasl oia sa gaoraond ron edmsnvskdat sohn oh hovhh lja do orono o foh osd erspsl inn i e h f ooldlt titcan entesn vthohw tsrv hedeca whios fo on

*aogtasv tdise ti ar aprl tu idtrt ao risvirk w rtpotr **old as** ta octtoeit a tsrsrtotdtannryot torptcodnoo mo osr ovoitd hortn ftud oodson r o nie"*

I then ran 600 epochs. After epoch 599, with seed = "homework for extra credit but luckily," my machine wrote

"u orrrn ev dr rdaupr rlwgnidt dindth ndj f dw ni de rb aldn lodnirtnarindet vrrono o tt dkdrrtoy e r w dd dlnetld p rrtirne ndoimefldnotddoucra ilili irlree daedbddecaada ttdng laddralr jtnifniry y addawaigrhya ngnt u duric wy ood ddrjrnhiaryouitlr ret ow aruei o rnntr adt c ir n wndo lir dl nfd idldderryd oslh srt w tdlln dddirerejo r r d oorid llriyi teis elddjn onp"

The one notable change was the larger words on average. Otherwise, I could not squeeze one 3-gram out of the entire endeavor.

I tested a few more models and concluded:

I do not have the machine power or time to train a model from scratch.

After several more hours of work, I decided to use a pre-trained **NN** model designed specifically for my purposes, a Text-Generating Neural Network, and to use Google's cloud services and GPU computing power to run the model. The code for training was surprisingly short, thanks to the work that others have done before me.

Here is the code

```
!pip install -q textgenrnn
from google.colab import files
from textgenrnn import textgenrnn
import os
model_cfg = {'rnn_size': 128,'rnn_layers': 4,'rnn_bidirectional':
True,
    'max_length': 40, 'max_words': 10000,  'dim_embeddings': 100,
    'word_level': False,
}
train_cfg = {'line_delimited': False,'num_epochs': 60,'gen_epochs':
2,
    'batch_size': 1024,'train_size': 0.8, 'dropout': 0.0,
    'max_gen_length': 500, 'validation': False, 'is_csv': False
}
## import Books1-10.txt here or your own text
model_name = 'colaboratory'
textgen = textgenrnn(name=model_name)
train_function = textgen.train_from_file if
train_cfg['line_delimited'] else textgen.train_from_largetext_file

train_function(file_path=latest_file, new_model=True,
    num_epochs=train_cfg['num_epochs'],
    gen_epochs=train_cfg['gen_epochs'],
    batch_size=train_cfg['batch_size'],
train_size=train_cfg['train_size'],
    dropout=train_cfg['dropout'],
     max_gen_length=train_cfg['max_gen_length'],
    validation=train_cfg['validation'], is_csv=train_cfg['is_csv'],
    rnn_layers=model_cfg['rnn_layers'],
    rnn_size=model_cfg['rnn_size'],
    rnn_bidirectional=model_cfg['rnn_bidirectional'],
    max_length=model_cfg['max_length'],
    dim_embeddings=model_cfg['dim_embeddings'],
    word_level=model_cfg['word_level'])
```

Here is the output (60 epoch, 3 hours later):

"Charlie got we bet it's time to go to the creaveys caught uncle laundry and he was up stature I really actually had seek me on a wedding he should start but I paid his mind rame darren and if Rowley let out after that until the boys did was todaing I'm out I just don t like something patty oooou at neountronina or celevaly back to school ad two months down the road me and Rowley start coming to the people behind us kids showed up at my whole week of plastic between me and Rowley have only

on as we took a locker and created any of my case tonight and got in their room i was pretty sure dad would tell them to get to call the milk but then mom said she'd be der the house waned out first the bed and managed the bag they anywhere because that s when i dropped it from school would we even confess so i got a junior o o on the police came to the floor she reads so udzt after all these years and he'd been looking forward to being stuck on at least grader who hitched up the back and they did

ven go nearby to see more shane Sunday the magic 8 ball aces health wave upstions I read driving the door in the s that could be a really tire so she let him how the end of practice aband no matter how much look but the pig was talking about but Mrs Dean hand that straight uncle joe my brother mom had taken a whole hunters after that and that since the womely are about everyone in town and the whole perpetrate feeling around the whole three-hour ended up well dad hate the whole perspires we"

Here is the output (120 epoch, 6 hours later):

"of deal of the least of all sorts of extra to imagine again conserving later goalizing with when she scraped she was going to end up with a bunch of soap and things up but kind of silas scratch trip as you in my ha a mark and some chocolate in the trash along the way things went kitting a well I knew where you're dropping drive for ketchup hand's for me and started the

three kicks coming from a a teacher were explaining kids home everybody s having a signed everyone knowing how many push-ups Tuesday

actually get a chance to hold in their books which was actually did of list that i can unformed mom's along so getting outside our neighborhood i thought mom is broken strange Tuesday when I got home from the water park today and the bike spanking through my chocolate chips Rodrick opening their auto and then started talking about her checking most exclushh-ummnated that i knew he just moved away typed the backstabbed me that did it upset and Rodrick with a bunch over the doggie day time zone

old print of the night so he could help us get devices went then cashier this year what it was pretty prawn Greg wet the ped typ space and figured the preventions now us to give mom had some laughed up Christmas with Rowley s family but we did a stop used bar so i started their minibar and whoever held to walk and that so much for the awesome and mama p s driveways when you re starting was still on the other end ep el in for the whole school year luckily mom found a called no matter how many note"

🜕

These are not perfect outputs, but substantially better than my first pass. Also, we did not include punctuation, which diminishes grammar constructs. Once we add the punctuation and capitalization back in, we could achieve an even better output.

Perhaps one day I'll do an entire book on teaching a machine to write a decent short story.

The endeavor was fun and several conclusions are worthy of note. First, I am not worried about machines competing with authors, yet. It is simple to mimic text; it is also simple to extrapolate above and beyond that initial baseline, to add to the mimicked text, but it's a different thing to generate a complete novel from scratch. The creative process is complex to duplicate or to teach. Creative writing is not a repetitive process, thus difficult to teach.

Second, I think dialogue would be very difficult to teach. As is, it is difficult to teach a human being to articulate thoughts, ideas, and feeling via spoken words. I cannot imagine it would be any easier to teach a machine.

For now, dear authors, your jobs are safe. But, save your money as the machines are getting better every day.

About the Author

Max Boroumand is a seasoned and experienced technologist, a futurist, and special advisor. His career spans over two decades, with clients in the Fortune 500, Governments, and non-profits, and many technology startups. His work and life have taken him all over the world, from the Middle East and North Africa, to Europe and the Americas, and to Asia.

Over the last decade, he has been the CEO of a holding company, whose portfolio includes several software companies, and most recently a publishing and media company supporting his new passion, writing books.

Coming Soon

A Machine's View: *Lord of the Ring Series*

A Machine's View: *Harry Potter Series*

Keep in Touch

www.boroumand.com

https://www.facebook.com/boroumand.MediArt/

https://twitter.com/boroumand

Made in the USA
Middletown, DE
14 April 2020